A
Grandparent's
Sorrow

by
Pat Schwiebert, RN
Director, Perinatal Loss / Grief Watch
Portland, Oregon

Illustrated by Jean Grover

Acknowledgments

I have been touched by the memorable grandparents who over the years have called just to talk about their incredible sense of loss at the death of their grandchild, and have shared their deep respect for their children who did what they needed to do to honor their dead babies. Some have written beautiful poems or letters... words that spoke from the heart their deep pain over the death of their grandchild.

I thank all of you, especially **Sharon Gates**, who would call with updates of how things were going; to **Carla Ritter**, who said, "I want to help make something available for grandparents so they don't have to feel so all alone;" to **Mary Williams**, because she just poured out her heart on paper, teaching her friends about the death of an infant and displaying a profound healing that can come from writing what's on your heart.

And finally, I thank my friend **Jean Grover**, who captured the grandparent's love for both the child and the grandchild with her striking illustrations.

Table Of Contents

Introduction

Your child's baby has died, and sorrow fills your lives in a way that you may not have experienced in the past. You grieve not only for the loss of your grandbaby that you will not get to enjoy growing up, but also for your child's loss in not being able to have what he or she wanted so much. It is a double loss for you, perhaps not as deep as the one your child will experience, but nonetheless significant, and in some ways more complicated.

A bereaved parent expressed her feelings like this. "I now feel older than my parents. I have experienced a major loss before they did." When this happens in your family, your child will become your teacher of grief. You will have to learn from your son or daughter what helps and what hurts, and what it feels like to live apart from a baby who could not live apart from its mother. And because your children don't know yet what they need, you will have to walk patiently and tenderly beside them.

This booklet is offered to you as a source of comfort, and also as a guideline to help you journey with your child during this difficult time.

*We weep for
that which would
have been
our delight.*

1

She was my third born – but my only daughter.
He was her first born – and so far, her only son.
The bond between us has lasted almost thirty years.
The bond between them lasted less than seven months.
Eric Thomas was born on September 1, 1992 – he died that same day.

There will never be a way to describe the intense pain I have felt for the past four days. I hope at no other time in my life will I experience such pain again. I have always known I loved my daughter – but never new how much until now. How precious she seems to me now – how scared it makes me feel to think of what I would do if I lost her.

As we held each other close and cried with such force that the room seemed to shake with our sobbing, I could only remember how much she had been wanted. I tried to imagine how I would have felt if she had never known this wonderful life, had never grown into a beautiful young woman, had never know the love of a wonderful man. I tried to imagine how I would have felt if I had lost her – but I couldn't. No one could feel the pain she was feeling at the loss of her beautiful son. And I felt totally helpless.

September 6, 1992
Carla Ritter, Eric's grandma

If one of your own babies died

If you experienced the death of one of your own babies during your childbearing years your grandchild's death may evoke a memory of your own hospital experience. You may be confused by the hospital personnel's way of dealing with your grandchild's death, probably very different from your own past experience.

There have been many changes in obstetric care over the last 20 years, one of them being how we now deal with perinatal bereavement. In the past we tended to diminish the death of a small infant and regarded it as a non event, assuming this approach would lessen the parent's suffering. We discouraged parents from seeing, holding, or even naming their baby. We have since learned by listening to parents that our well meaning advice was misguided. We now confront and acknowledge the death of a baby as the human tragedy that it is and help parents find ways to say goodbye to their little one.

Sometimes, when our children choose to do something in a way different from what we chose, we think that their choice is a reflection on us or a rejection of our values. It's important to remember that the ways your children have chosen to deal with the loss of their baby were most likely not options when your baby died.

You may also find yourself regretting not having had the same opportunities provided you to mourn your dead baby. Watching your child do what you wished you had to opportunity to do may evoke strong emotions in you.

Both of these reactions are common. How you react can interfere with your being able to be helpful to your children right now.

Being honest with your child about how your grandbaby's death is affecting you will help them understand your reactions. But it will also be essential for you to remember that this is your child's experience, not yours, and you are an invited guest at this very intimate time.

There was a Time

There was a time when I could make it all better.
That time is no more.
I could kiss your hurts
and mend them in an instant.
I could wipe away your tears
and see your beautiful smile return to your face.
And when your hopes were dashed
I could help you find a reason not to give up.
But that was when
the world only knew you as a fresh young rose.
That was when
life was sweet
and the worst thing that ever
happened was
a broken heart,
from the boy next door.
There was a time
when I could make it all better.
That time is no more.

A Picture of Grief

Grief is so very unique. There are lots of similarities in the ways that individuals grieve, but there is no single, consistent pattern of grief that fits everyone. Nor is there any perfect formula for moving through the grief process. Age, previous live experiences, personal coping skills, availability and adequacy of a support system, physical and emotional health, and the presence or absence of other life stresses will all be woven into the fabric of any one given experience.

Nor is there anything constant about grief. Grief changes its face from day to day, and even from hour to hour. Mostly you will find this variation to be a relief, but it can sometimes catch you off guard and be bewildering.

Don't be surprised if your child's grief manifests itself in any of the ways described below:

• At first your children, and you as well, may progress through a variety of confusing emotions with little warning. Only later will you begin to develop a little more control.

• Your child may go through a period of hibernation and seclusion.

• Your child may have an impulse to tell everyone about their loss, including complete strangers.

• Your children's marriage may appear to be on rocky ground because the two of them are processing their grief in very different ways.

• Your child may fear returning to work or may lose interest in hobbies or other activities that he or she had previously enjoyed.

• Your daughter may resent seeing other pregnant women and/or be jealous when a friend gets pregnant.

• Your child may become short tempered and have little patience with trivial things.

• Your daughter especially may want to avoid family gatherings where other children are present and having a good time.

• Your child may be very fearful that she will forget what her child looked like, and even more importantly, that others will forget that the baby even existed.

Playing the role of parent to a grieving adult child will be both a blessing and a curse as you try to figure out how you can be most helpful in any given situation. Because you will be eager to do the right thing, and fearful of doing harm, you may find that you are often timid in your responses. You will experience moments of affectionate caring and times of bittersweet emotional pain.

It is tempting for us to want to live in this world without having to suffer. And certainly that is what we desire for our children. We would like to protect our children from having to experience the distress that we have encountered. I have heard mothers say they would gladly go through labor for their daughters if they could, so that their daughters would not have to experience the pain of labor. Such is the desire to protect the child from what the mother feels as the harshness or unfairness of life. But even if such protection were possible, it would deny to your daughters the gifts that are abundant in the experience of *giving birth to themselves* as they give birth to their children. The same is true with the experience of a deep loss, such as losing a baby. We would like to believe that if we don't talk about the loss, minimize it, or even deny any significant impact, then we wont have to deal with the emotional problems that it presents. But truly it is a willingness to be drawn to the depth of despair that will allow our children to grow and mature emotionally and spiritually.

We try in vain to protect our children from the agony of death and grief. A wise parent, however, learns to trust the child's ability to swim in the sea of grief without drowning. That same parent knows that the child can only become fully alive by being submerged in the depths of his or her own sorrow, by experiencing the death and hell that is a part of grief, and finally by being restored to life as

6

one forever changed.

How can we help our children maintain their rightful role as parents in this situation when we're tempted to assume the parental role, thereby keeping them dependent on us?

How do we help them accomplish this? By being present with our children. By modeling how to be a parent, and by affirming our trust in their ability to do the hardest thing they may ever have to do. By reminding them that there is something within them that will guide them and nurture them, just as we were guided and nurtured during the difficult times in our lives.

Love calls me to places
I would not ordinarily go.
The landscapes of desire so barren
and dark
stripped naked and raw,
this heart burst open, bleeds
into infinity
of unrequited longing
-bell hooks

Once I Turned Fifty

Once I turned fifty I was ready to be a grandma.
 It seemed that I had just enough energy
  almost enough wisdom
  and plenty of love
   that I had been saving up to
   give to this new little person.
I always wondered what it would be like.
 Would I love her as much as I loved you when
   you were first born?
    (I think I do.)
Would I spend hours holding her like I held you,
  gazing into your eyes,
   telling you secrets
   and dreaming of what our life would be like
    together?
    (I wish I could.)
Would she look like you
  or resemble her dad?
   (a bit of both of you, I think.)
Would she break my heart like you could do?
    Yes.

Pat Schwiebert

People ask
what is the
meaning of
your arms
folded
over
your
chest.
Are you
mad?
Are you
protecting
yourself?
Does
your
heart
hurt?
Yes.
Yes.
Yes.
And I
remember
feeling
strong
and proud and scared
when I first held
my child,
and
thought that I
would always protect her.
What can I do now?
All our arms are empty.

J.G.

9

About the Hospital Experience

As we suggested earlier, you may be surprised and even appalled at the very frank and open way the hospital staff communicates to your child following the death of their baby. Especially if your tendency is to want to be over-protective of your child by minimizing the reality of the loss, you may view the approach of the staff as being somewhat cruel and contrary to what you perceive to be in the best interest of your child. But we have found that the most compassionate care we can offer includes helping the bereaved parents to confront rather than deny the severity of their loss. This approach may seem incongruent with what you have understood to be the objective of the healing arts because this kind of care doesn't protect your child from pain. But it will give them opportunities to say hello and good-bye to their baby in ways, which they will be able to remember with positive feelings down the road. And it will help them with the essential skills and tools to take with them on their healing journey.

There is precious little time for the hospital staff to prepare your child for the grief that lies ahead. The maternity ward or an area nearby is the ideal place to begin this process toward a healing mainly because the staff is usually trained to deal with situations like this. Hiding your child from the reality that she is indeed a parent, by having her cared for by personnel who are not trained in obstetrics, denies her important information she needs about caring for her body after she goes home. It also denies her and her partner the opportunity to see and hear other babies, which though sometimes difficult, can be an important part of the healing process. And it is better that this happen initially with a caring staff around than to face it alone later.

*Your grief will probably not last
as long as will your child's grief.
However, your concern for your
child will last as long as their grief does.*

10

Nothing to say, we turn away.

How to Help Your Child

1. Offer to stay at the hospital with your child and his/her partner, but also assure them of your willingness to honor their privacy if that is what they prefer. Don't wait until they invite you to stay, however. They may be trying to protect you by not suggesting that you come, when in fact your presence is what they most desire.

2. Take your camera to record pictures of the baby, of your children holding their child, and of you holding your grandchild. Ask the nurse to take a family picture of all of you. Have the pictures developed, but let your children decide when they want to see them. Don't assume they will want to see them right away. Don't discard any of the pictures just because you think they aren't good enough. Also, it's better not to show the pictures to anyone else without your child's permission. If your child offers you a picture of your grandchild, consider displaying it with the pictures of your other grandchildren.

3. Offer the parents an opportunity to spend time alone with their child.

4. Don't go to your child's home and begin to rearrange the room, which was set up as the nursery for your new grandchild. This is something the bereaved parents will probably need to do as a part of their grieving process. You may be asked to do it with them later, but they need to decide if and when. Don't worry if they wait longer than you think they should before beginning to rearrange the room.

5. Buy your daughter a new outfit so she won't have to wear maternity clothes home from the hospital.

6. If there are other grandchildren in the family, offer to provide respite care for them.

7. Run errands and provide food

8. Save the dried flowers from bouquets that were sent to your children and fill clear glass Christmas ornaments with the petals, or make potpourri or some other treasure for them.

9. Later, when anyone asks you how many grandchildren you have, be sure to include your dead grandchild in the total.

10. Always mention your dead grandchild by name, just as you would any other grandchild.

11. Remember your child on Mother's Day, Father's Day, and other holidays. Observing holidays may be especially hard for them. Your acknowledgement to them of the possibility of it being a difficult time may help ease the pain somewhat.

12. If prayers are offered at family gatherings, acknowledge the absence of the dead child in your prayer, just as you would any other member of the family who has recently died.

13. Send your child notes that let her know you haven't forgotten.

14. Take her out to lunch.

15. Bring up the subject of your grandbaby from time to time. If your child doesn't want to talk about it, she won't. But it helps her to know that you are thinking of the baby too, and that you don't mind talking about the infant who died.

16. Avoid telling your child what he/she should do.

17. Encourage your child and his/her partner to find a grief support group so they can talk with others who have experienced the death of a baby, too. Though you may be a wonderful sounding board for your children, they (and you) will probably benefit from an expansion of their support system.

18. Remember, the grief process will take much longer than you want it to.

What Not to Say

"The child wouldn't have been healthy."
"What did you do wrong?"
"You're young; you can always have more
children."
"It was meant to be."
"At least you have other children."
"Maybe next time you'll take better care of
yourself."
"Life goes on."
"You aren't going to go to the same doctor next
time, are you?"
"Try to get pregnant as soon as you can."
"You've got to be strong."
"Don't cry. Everything is going to be all right."
"Can't we talk about something else?"
"Just be glad you didn't get to know the baby. Then
you'd really be sad."
"It was only a miscarriage."
"I know just how you feel."
"It won't happen again."
"I understand."

What to Say Instead

"I don't know what to say, but I'll be glad to listen."
"You must feel terrible."
"Tell me about it."
"Is there anything I can do to help?"
"Help me to know how I can best be there for you."

14

How to Take Care of Yourself

1. Allow yourself to cry. Cry hard if you need to, but try not to cry harder than your children do while in their presence. To do so may put them in the position of thinking they have to take care of you. It's good for them to be able to see you cry, though. It gives them permission to cry also, especially if they have grown up feeling that it's not okay for an adult to cry. It also lets them know you care about the baby, too.

2. Find someone to talk to, such as another grandparent who has lost a child. You'll be amazed at how quickly you'll connect with such persons when you let others know what has happened to you.

3. Write your feelings in a journal.

4. Get plenty of sleep. Grief is both emotionally and physically exhausting.

5. Exercise. This helps to release the stress built up in grief.

6. Read about grief so you can understand it better.

7. Don't deny your own feelings in order to take care of your child.

*I have two grandsons
and two granddaughters.
One grandson lives in Tucson
with his mom and dad.
The other grandson and his sister
live with their parents in New York.
I now have a grandchild
who lives in my heart.
How many do you have?*

Gifts to Give Your Grieving Child

The following are some gifts that may serve as ways of helping your children remember their baby.

- a rosebush or tree
- flowers for the altar of your church – on the anniversary of your grandchild's birth and death
- a book for the local library in memory of your grandchild
- a locket – engrave the baby's name and birthday on the front and put a picture or lock of hair inside
- a charm (i.e. heart, star, or angel) that could hold the baby's birthstone
- a memory album
- a journal
- an urn to hold the child's ashes
- a picture frame
- a special box to hold memorabilia
- a poem which you have written
- a journal of memories, which you have kept, to be given later
- a quilt which you have made
- a Christmas ornament
- a warm shawl because grief can make you stone cold inside
- a musical tape to help get to the passion of their grief
- money, or maybe a phone card because grief can be very costly in many different ways

Faithful indeed
is the spirit
that remembers

If Your Child had a Multiple Pregnancy

It is tempting, in the case of a multiple pregnancy, to want to dismiss the importance of the child who died and to focus only on the baby that survived. But try not to forget that the parents are grieving the loss of the other child at the same time they are trying to enjoy their experience with the surviving twin.

Refer to the surviving child as a twin, and don't hesitate to talk about the child that died. Give the parents time off from parenting the surviving child so they can take time to mourn the one that died. And on every birthday anniversary, remember to speak about the one who isn't there.

Many people regard a multiple pregnancy as very special. And even though some of us groan at the thought of having to care for more than one baby at a time, still there is great pride in being unique. So when one of the babies died, you not only lose the baby, you also lose the distinction of being the parent of twins, triplets, etc.

If Your Child Interrupted the Pregnancy for Medical Reasons

Because of the latest medical technologies, we are now able to know when an unborn child is unlikely to survive. Parents are now given the option to terminate the pregnancy rather than continue the pregnancy to term and then watch the baby die. For some, this is a very controversial and problematic choice. Your children need your compassion and support in making this very difficult decision. Certain other people may be very judgmental about the termination of any pregnancy, making it difficult for the parents to explain why the baby died. "Secrets" may imply to some people that the pregnant parents have done something wrong and this may further complicate the parent's grief. Stand by your child's decision. Be careful not to infer that they did the wrong thing. And don't assume that they won't need to go through a process of grief just because they made the decision to hasten the baby's birth and inevitable death. Honor this grandchild just like you would if the baby had died another way.

Dealing with Friends

You have probably already told friends that you are expecting a grandchild. Now you're going to have to tell them something that will be difficult to say because to say it is to confront again the reality of your loss. You may find that you can't hold back tears when you say the words, "My grandchild died." The reactions you get from friends may vary greatly. Some will be supportive and encourage you to talk, and others may be embarrassed by your tears and quickly try to change the subject. Some who have heard the news from someone else may tend to avoid you for a while. Death and grief do funny things to people.

Infant loss for many people is considered a non-event. Your friends may be surprised that you or your children are making such a fuss over this little person whom no one even knew. After all, in years past people didn't make a big deal about infant loss. And you may find your friends, and even family members, shocked to learn that your children actually held the baby, took pictures of the dead infant, and held a memorial service for the child. Be sure to explain to them that doing these things has proven to be more beneficial than the ways of earlier generations.

It is natural for people to want to be comforted and acknowledged for what they are going through. Your children need this opportunity and so do you. If your friends are unaware of the needs of the bereaved and are making assumptions based on their own discomfort (i.e. "I don't want to talk about it, so you probably don't want to either," or "the less said the better"), you may have to coach them on what you need. You may have to initiate the conversation yourself.

Try to be patient with your friends, remembering that you may have just become aware of some of this "grief stuff," too. You may also be doing them a real favor by providing them with information, which will help them deal with grief in their own family at some future time.

Your Faith may be Challenged

Many people who experience a tragedy as devastating as the death of a child cannot help wondering how a compassionate and loving God could allow such a terrible thing to happen. If you are such a person, you needn't worry or feel guilty because of your feelings, which are really quite normal and natural.

The experience of many bereaved parents and grandparents we have known is that, following an initial period characterized by anger toward God and/or mistrust of God, they begin to experience a new level of faith, a faith that is less naïve and more able to withstand the challenge of extreme grief and loss. What these parents and grandparents have discovered is that the power of God is not the power to prevent tragedies, many of which are the indirect result of our negligence and abuse as a human race. Rather, the power of God is the power of love to heal our grief and to console us as we wait with God and work with God in that healing process.

Many of the Biblical Psalms can be a source of comfort for those who are grieving. They are honest expressions of the anger, frustration, fear, and other emotions experienced by those who have suffered because of personal loss and systemic oppression.

You may want to read these Psalms and discover in them the ways that the writer is able to move from uncertainty to faith, and from anger to gratitude.

When you pray, do not hesitate to speak your deepest feelings, even though they are expressions of doubt and a loss of faith. We come

19

nearest to the heart of God when we communicate honestly, and God, who suffers with us in our pain, can be a wonderful ally in the healing process.

Dear God,

You and I have been through some pretty rough times together. There have been times when I wondered where in the world you were when I was having trouble. I expected you to come and protect me from the bad things that were happening. But the bad things happened anyway. Somehow, the relationship you have with my daughter is different.

When Cheryl got pregnant and then we found out that the baby was encephalic I thought for sure you had deserted me and my family.

The doctors wanted Cheryl to terminate the pregnancy but she refused. Even when they told her that the child would be born without a brain Cheryl refused to budge on her decision. She kept telling the doctors, "We believe in miracles. How can there be a miracle if we don't give God a chance?"

I didn't know how to help her. The doctors wanted me to persuade her that the best thing would be for the baby to be born now.

The baby was born just a few weeks before her due date. She wasn't at all unsightly like they said she might be. We put on her not-so-perfect head a special little bonnet we had made for her. We took her home and loved her to death three days later. This baby changed many peoples lives and softened many hardened hearts. That was miracle enough for us.

Sharon Gates

When I know that life
is a mystery,
I don't need reasons.
And I know that death
is a mystery –
but God, give me reasons.
J.G.

My head is like a solid rock
I feel no pain.
My eyes see the glory
of God.
My ears hear the voice
of angels.
My nose smells the fragrance of
flowers in the garden.
My mouth tastes the fruit
Of the spirit.

by grandma
Sharon Gates

21

Although we know that after such a loss the acute stage of mourning will subside, we also know that we shall remain inconsolable and will never find a substitute. No matter what may fill the gap, even if it be filled completely, it nevertheless remains something else. And actually, this is how it should be. It is the only way of perpetuating that love which we do not want to relinquish.

Sigmund Freud

Talking with your Grandchildren

Your surviving grandchildren need to be told that they have a brother or sister and that the baby died. How to tell the surviving child and how to help the child participate in the immediate experience will depend on the child's age, the child's communication skills, and the parent's level of coping.

In most cases, your grandchild will benefit from having a chance to see and hold the baby. The important thing here is to prepare the grandchild ahead of time for what the baby will look and feel like. If the grandchild doesn't seem interested in seeing the baby, she should not be forced to do so. Showing the grandchild pictures of the baby or other mementos of the baby's short life, at some later time when the child is curious, will provide tangible evidence of the baby's life.

A small child is more disturbed by disruptions in his life, (e.g. people around him talking in hushed tones or crying, being suddenly cared for by strangers, not having the attention of a parent who is too consumed by grief to be able to attend to the normal care-giving role) than by the death of the baby itself. Most small children find it much easier to deal with the sadness experienced by the adults in their live than with the emotional withdrawal of those they normally look to to meet their comfort needs. The small child needs to be offered reassurance that he has not been forgotten during this confusing and difficult time.

Sometimes we may want to avoid talking with our grandchildren because we're afraid we may say the wrong thing, or because we don't know how to explain death. None of us needs to feel alone in this struggle. The most important thing to remember is that it is okay not to have all the answers. If you explain death in a way that you later decide must have been confusing or inadequate, you can always bring up the subject again at a later time.

The choice of words in describing death is very important. It is better to not use euphemisms for death. If a child is told that his brother is "asleep," he could confuse sleep with death and later develop a sleep disorder related to his fears of death. Another generalization to avoid is this one: "God loved the baby so much that God took the baby to heaven to be with God." The surviving child may decide it is safer to act "bad" so he won't have to worry about leaving his parents. Saying the baby went away is also confusing because it contributes to the belief that the baby will return someday.

Remember that young children believe in magic, and the concept of something being permanent alludes their understanding. Don't be afraid if the child asks a lot of questions, sometimes the same question many times. It's almost like if they keep asking the same question, they'll finally get the answer they want. And don't worry if, in his play, the child pretends that he or someone else is dead. This is all very normal. The more we show our children and grandchildren that we are able to talk about death openly, the more they are likely to share openly what they are feeling. Our grandchildren will not have to grow up with the belief that death is a forbidden subject.

Your children will probably receive cards, flowers and gifts acknowledging their grief from friends and relatives. You may want to send your grandchildren a card letting them know you are thinking of them too, or give a gift that will help them in their grieving time. This will help your grandchildren feel like part of a grieving family.

"Grandma, what is that?"
"It's a mortuary. It's a place where we take people when they die."
"If I die, will you take me there?"
"Yes, probably."
"Will you come back and get me in a few days and take me home?"

A List of Books You can Read to Your Grandchildren

Books available through Grief Watch

The following books are all available through Grief Watch. While their are many other places that stock them as well, Grief Watch lists a wide variety of books so that it is easier to find the right one for you and your family. For more information visit www.griefwatch.com.

- We Were Gonna Have A Baby, But We Had An Angel Instead, by Pat Schwiebert

- Angel with the Golden Glow, by Elissa Al-Chokhachy

- Where's Jess, by Joy and Marv Johnson

- An Angel in the Sky, by Sheila Booth-Alberstadt

- No New Baby, by Marilyn Gryte

- The Secret of the Dragonfly, by Gayle Shaw-Cramer and Jan Jones

- Someone Came Before You, by Pat Schwiebert

- After a Death, an Activity Book for Children, by Dougy Center Staff

- When Dinosaurs Die, a Guide to Understanding Death, by Laurie Krasny Brown and Marc Brown

- Aarvy Aardvark Finds Hope, by Donna Toole

- What is Dead?, by Heather Lawrence

- A Complete Book About Death for Kids, by Earl Grollman and Joy Johnson

- Straight Talk About Death for Teenagers, by Earl Grollman

25

Other recommended books

Most of these books should be available in the children's section of your local library or bookstore, or can be found and ordered online.

Badger's Parting Gifts, by Susan Varley

About Dying, by Sara Stein

It Must Hurt a Lot, by Doris Sanford

I'll Always Love You, by Hans Wilhelm

Lifetimes, by Mellonie and Ingpen

The Tenth Good Thing About Barney, by Judith Viorst

Wilford Gordon McDonald Partridge, by Mem Fox

The Fall of Freddie the Leaf, by Leo Buscalgia

All of the books listed have been highly recommended by parents. Your local children's bookstore may also be able to help you locate the most recent books published for children on the subject of death, dying, and grief. A quick search online is another great way to learn about new or popular children's grief books.

Stillborn, such an ugly word (to me at least), has always meant still to be born. As if awaiting an event that hasn't happened yet. Not for me, that word.

Born dead. That's what happened. Our grandson Jason was born dead. Two words, two events.

Born. Yes, Jason was born. We were there. His parents, sister, aunt, myself, all clad in our blue hospital scrubs. The "cheering team" for this long awaited joyous event gathered in the birthing room.

Dead, yes, born dead. They tried, those wonderful medical team members. They did all they knew how to do, but the cord had been too long around his neck. An accident, an unforeseeable, unavoidable accident snuffed out our baby's life before he could say hello to our world. Dead, but not gone from us. We cry together, we love together, hold our beloved little one together. Croon to him the words we've been waiting to say. Grieve for all the things we will never do with this child. He looks so peaceful, as if he will awaken at any moment and cry. We want so badly to hear this sound, but no, it's not meant to be. He sleeps, the eternal sleep. He is with God, another angel in the heavens. That's little solace now. God has enough angels, we think. God made a mistake, we think.

We leave. Mother and father need time alone with their son. The need time to say hello to Jason Alan, even though it means good-bye.

Time for decisions. The hospital offers to dispose of the body, if we wish. Respectfully, certainly, but no, thank you, not for us. Even though Jason never walked the path of life and left no footprints in the sand, he lived. We will always carry him in our hearts. We feel his little footprints though.

The parents, together, in their sorrow decide. "Our son will wear his christening gown and lie upon his blanket in his cradle, all hand-made and chosen with love, to greet all who come to the chapel to share our sorrow. Hello may mean good-bye, but they will at least meet our beloved baby boy. "So beautiful, so peaceful, so loved."

Father comes, a kindly priest, with gentle words and sparkling eyes. A rosebud, says Father. Picked before it could bloom. Such a beautiful thought. Pink and perfect in itself. We treasure a rosebud for its unique beauty. Jason is our own rosebud. Picked before his time.

Our last good-bye. We hold him, cradle him, croon to him for the last time.

Mom and dad stay behind. They need more time to say their farewell. We try to fill their needs with our love and support of how they want things done. I thank God we are together, gathered here by our need to share. We need each other.

I, the grandmother, carry Jason's ashes "home" across the country to the family home where all of us will eventually come.

A special garden is designated as Jason's. A beautiful spot chosen by his father that has slowly grown over the years between the fruit orchard and tree house. Strangely, it has had no name, unlike other areas on the place, and now it does. A marker will be made, a birdbath placed. Some miniature roses will be added. All labors of love to remind us of a child who touched our hearts and our lives. Ever so briefly, but never to be forgotten.

We have five grandchildren, my husband and I. One of them is an angel. Jason was born dead and we love him in a special way.

Jason Alan Yeager
January 17, 1988 9:12 PM
8 lb. 3 oz. 21 ¾ inches.
Mary Williams
Jason's grandma

*What we
remember
lives on…*

28

*Grief has the potential
to bring out
the best and the worst
in people.*

You're not helping!

Here's how you can help me:
Don't try to fix me.
Let me be sad.
Trust me to know how to grieve.
Mention my loved one's name.
Let me cry.
Help me remember.

additional resources available at www.griefwatch.com

If You and Your Child Don't have a Good Relationship Right Now

All advice you have read so far will work best for families who communicate well at this time in their lives. We recognize not all families are able to do this, for one reason or another. We offer some advice here that may help to minimize conflict and hurt feelings in a difficult family situation.

1. Remember that your children are extremely vulnerable right now. When speaking to them, be especially cautious about the words you choose.

2. Some daughters who have struggled to break away from the influence of their mothers may be afraid to accept their mother's sincere offer to help for fear of losing the independence they have gained. The sense of a daughter's rejection may hurt you, but trust her process. Give her the space she needs by not hovering. You must resist your innate desire to "fix" things. Being an interfering mother or mother-in-law is not what she and her partner need. It is important that you let them work through the grief themselves – and you MUST let them.

3. Some adult children have difficulties with an in-law, and some in-laws have difficulties with their child's spouse. A death in the family tends to magnify such problems rather than diminish them. Acknowledging the rift is quite appropriate, e.g. "I know things aren't right between us right now, but I'm here for you if you need me."

4. Dropping a note in the mail or leaving a message on the answering machine will help reassure your children that you haven't forgotten them. At the same time, it will reduce the risk of communication problems that may occur in a conversation. Tell them they don't need to respond, that you just called to let them know you are thinking of them.

5. It is better that you not talk with other member of the family about how your children are going about their grief work... especially if you don't agree with their process. Reports of such conversations will most likely get back to your children and they will tend to feel that they are being watched and gossiped about.

6. You may "do it wrong," and the chances are good that you will do something "wrong." This most likely will happen not because you don't care, but because your children are emotionally vulnerable and they have a diminished capacity to tolerate anything they see as insensitive. It will also happen because you are only human and most likely working in unfamiliar territory. If you do make a mistake, just tell them you're sorry and move on. Try not to dwell on the mistakes.

7. Find someone who can be a good listener for you. A counselor may be helpful. Or maybe you will want to confide in a good friend who understands grief and is aware of the strained relationship between you and your child, but can remain objective. It helps to have a safe place to let your feelings out so they don't fester and get blown out of proportion.

Never give up the
opportunity to
keep your mouth shut.

Grandmother's Rights

Grandmotherhood
does not give
us the right to
speak without thinking.
But only the right to
think without speaking.

I didn't want those
I love
to see my pain; I
wanted to be their strength.
I didn't want them to feel
the powerlessness that comes
with witnessing loved one's
wounds.
But when I was all alone
I let the sorrow
that filled my heart flow
and the cat
came
with its
rough tongue
and lapped up
my salty tears.

I can see him laughing
I can see him loving
I can see him playing
* this son of mine.*

All I need to do is close my eyes
and see the two of them
*   hand in hand*
heading for their next adventure.
But this dream will have to wait
* till my next grandchild comes along.*

Pat Schwiebert

When Your Children Decide to Try Again

The desire for your children to fill the hole in their hearts may be a strong force for you and your children. Resist the sincere desire to make things better by encouraging them to try again too soon. This tends to minimize the baby that just died and makes it sound like they can replace the dead baby with another child.

When your kids do get pregnant, even though the odds are on their side that everything will go well, it will be hard to convince them that it won't happen again. 'Cause it wasn't supposed to happen the first time. Superstition and irrational thinking are common themes even in the most educated of bereaved parents.

Make sure you get approval from your children that it's okay to let others know of the next pregnancy. They may be very cautious about telling others and may want to make sure the baby is viable before sharing the news with others.

Note the time in the last pregnancy when things went bad. This is likely to be an anxious time during their next pregnancy also. Let them know you remember. Due dates and birth dates of the baby that died are important dates to keep in mind also.

Encourage them. Listen to their fears. Let them talk about the one that has died as they need to.

Be excited for your children, but don't forget the one that came before.

An Afterthought

Her heart quivered with conflicting emotions as she felt their resistance to her persistent nudging. "Why does the thrill of soaring have to begin with the fear of falling?" she thought. The ageless question was still unanswered for her.

As in the tradition of the species, her nest was located high on the shelf of a sheer rock face. Below there was nothing but air to support the wings of each child. "Is it possible that this time it will not work?" she thought. Despite her fears, the eagle knew it was time. Her parental mission was all but complete. There remained one final task – the push.

The eagle drew courage from an innate wisdom. Until her children discovered their wings, there was no purpose for their lives. Until they learned how to soar, they would fail to understand the privilege it was to have been born an eagle. The push was the greatest gift she could offer. It was her supreme act of love. And so one by one, she pushed them out, and they flew.

The Brown Star Story

Not long ago, astronomers found in the heavens gaseous celestial bodies—clouds of cosmic dust—which they think have finally answered the mystery of what exists between the small things in the universe, like planets, and the bigger things, like the sun. They call this cosmic dust "brown dwarfs" or "prestars," because, although brown dwarfs have all the same elements to become a star, for some reason they never did.

Most stars go on to live full lives, from their hot, bright white dwarf stage to their aged, cooler and dimmer red giant stage. But "brown stars" only go so far. Instead of being born to live a normal star's life, they remain cool and dim, hiding in the heavens, sprinkled in clusters among the other stars, 150 light years from Earth.

But, like our babies, their roles in the universe are very important. In fact, scientists believe they serve as a link between the small things and the big things, holding the universe together. A mid-point between the beginning and ending of our universal story.

As we grieve our babies who died before reaching the stardom of their earthly lives, perhaps we can find comfort in the possibility that they were designated for this very special universal role. Energized by our love, they are guardians of our memories of what was and our dreams of what some day may be.

As we look to the heavens seeking answers, we send messages of love to our "brown star" babies.

~Kim Steffgen

Additional Resources from Grief Watch

Heart Prints
These handmade ceramic hearts were first introduced with the option of a handprint or footprint (in blue or pink), but have now been broadened to include angel, butterfly, dragonfly, cross or paw print (only available in white). They are a nice way to say "I remember."

The Remembering Heart
Two beautiful handcrafted ceramic hearts in one. When separated, the tiny inner heart can be placed with the loved one who has died as a reminder of their unbroken connection to those who remain behind. They can also be tied together to form a necklace of love around the loved one. The outer heart is kept by the bereaved and can be worn on a necklace, acknowledging their grief.

Hole in My Heart
A simple brightly colored ceramic heart with a hole in it. Made for those who want to show that they are not "complete" and that someone very special is missing in their life.

Support Cards
A pack of 100 questions or statements that are a great way to start a conversation after a death. Draw a card at dinner and see where the conversation goes. Some examples are: "What is the hardest part of my grief?" "What am I learning about myself as I grieve?" and "How does my grief affect my daily life and activities?"

Rainbow Butterfly Plaque
"What the caterpillar calls the end of life, the Master calls the butterfly" is the inscribed in purple ink above this rainbow colored butterfly. The butterfly image comes mounted on an 8x10-inch frame matte board in the color of your choice. A great way to add a little color and a positive message to any room.

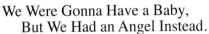

We Were Gonna Have a Baby, But We Had an Angel Instead.

A children's book told from a young child's perspective about the excitement and dreams of a coming baby, and the disappointment and sadness of a miscarriage. Beautiful ink and watercolor illustrations.

Someone Came Before You

A book for the child who comes after a sibling who died. It's a perfect gift just for them. It explains in a gentle way the parents' desire for a child and the sadness that comes over them when that baby dies. Includes suggestions about keeping your baby's memory alive.

Tear Soup, a recipe for healing after a loss

One of the most unique aspects of Tear Soup is that it speaks to every generation while demonstrating the universality of grief. If you are new to grief, Tear Soup will help you to understand the issues that grief presents. If you are bereaved, you will feel understood. The "tips" section in the back of the book is rich with wisdom and concrete recommendations. 56 pages of beautiful, heartfelt illustrations.

When Hello Means Goodbye

This sensitive booklet is a help to families during the early days of their grief. It helps answer questions and prepare parents for the days ahead. Among topics covered are: collecting keepsakes; ways to celebrate the birth and death of a baby; reasons for seeing, holding and naming a dead baby; emotions common to bereaved parents; information about autopsies; and where to find help.

Strong and Tender

A book especially for fathers, this is a collection of insights, helpful hints and tender thoughts to give a father strength during the dark times of grief following his baby's death. For too long fathers have been the forgotten grievers. By giving him this special book you tell him you also recognize his loss.

Still to be Born

Addresses the needs of the couple who are still longing for a baby, but afraid of being hurt again. Among the many topics covered in this 120-page book are: Why mourn the loss of someone you never knew? How soon should you attempt another pregnancy? and What are the chances of the same thing happening again?

Personalized Items from Grief Watch

Comfee Doll
For those lonely times when your arms are aching for something to hold. Heat this flannel-covered friend in the microwave for three minutes and it will stay warm for up to an hour. Contains flax and calming lavender. You can also have your grandbaby's name embroidered around the heart on your comfee's chest. Available in a wide variety of colors and patterns (solid colors strongly recommended for embroidered dolls).

Certificate of Life
Delicately embossed, with iridescent stars, flowers and a weeping teddy bear, these cream colored certificates acknowledge both the death and life of your baby. Available style options are Miscarriage, Stillborn and Neonatal Loss. A way to remember this baby was real, was wanted, was loved.

Angel T-Shirt
The saying "Some people only dream of angels. I held one in my arms." surrounded by gold stars, is silk-screened onto a 100% cotton T-shirt. These shirts can be embroidered with your grandbaby's name around the topmost star. Your choice of t-shirt color includes black, navy blue, purple or red.

Singing Ornaments
Imagine your loved one cradled in a star or by an angel. Our textured white ceramic ornaments make soft clinking sound whenever they move. They can be used as a holiday ornament, a wind-chime, or as a remembering gift to loved ones. Available ornaments include Angel, Heart, Star, Butterfly, Dragonfly, Bell or Tree. You can also personalize you Singing Ornament by adding a birthstone to the heart or star at its center.

For ordering information visit: www.griefwatch.com

Notes

Notes